MW00906972

COPYRIGHT

For more great titles visit
www.SmartWordBooks.com

DID YOU KNOW...

Although dolphins have small ears scientists believe that dolphins pick up sounds in their lower jaw, which then travels up to their inner ear and brain.

Dolphins can hear an underwater sound from 15 miles away.

Even though dolphins can swim to great depths they like to spend their time in shallow water.

There are reportedly 41 species of dolphin. 36 live in the ocean and the other 5 live in fresh water.

As a way of saving energy some dolphins swim closely alongside boats. Known as "Bow Riding" this type of swimming allows the dolphins to be pulled along by the ships current.

Scientists aren't sure why dolphins jump out of water. It could be to save energy, get a better view, impress others or to clean themselves, we're just not sure.

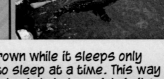

So a dolphin doesn't drown while it sleeps only half of its brain goes to sleep at a time. This way the active half of their brain help to maintain its breathing and swimming.

Dolphins can vary in length from 4 to 20 feet.

Dolphins are fast healers and can survive deep wounds that would kill other sea creatures.

Dolphins at sea get their water supply from their food rather than from sea water. Sea water is too salty for them to drink and can make them very sick.

Like humans some dolphins have been known to suffer from diabetes.

A fully grown dolphin has 100 teeth in their mouth. But while dolphins have teeth they don't have any jaw muscles so they don't chew their food but swallow it whole.

Dolphins carry more oxygen in their blood than other fish in the sea.

Only one tablespoon of water in a dolphin's lung can drown it. This is incredible when you consider that a human being can drown when 2 tablespoon of water enters their lungs.

A dolphin's blow hole was originally a nose that moved further up their face as they evolved.

A dolphin can speak in whistles and clicks at the same time. That's the equivalent of a human being having two conversations with two different voices at the exact same time.

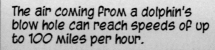

The air coming from a dolphin's blow hole can reach speeds of up to 100 miles per hour.

While some dolphins need to breathe every 20 seconds, other ones can get away with taking a breath every half an hour.

Dolphins use tools just like humans do. To protect their noses from damage while foraging some dolphins hold a sea sponge in their mouth.

Some dolphins can make up to 1,000 clicking sounds in just 1 second.

The name dolphin comes from a Greek word meaning "womb".

Some dolphins have been known to stay with and help injured whales. Even going as far as to push them to the surface of the water to help them breathe.

While fish swim by moving their tails sideways, dolphins swim through the water by moving their tails up and down.

When fishing dolphins herd the shoal of fish into a tight ball and then take turns swimming through the middle grabbing fish as they go.

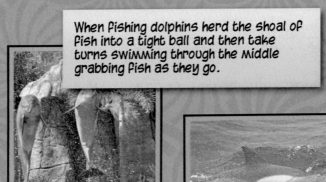

If a dolphin was given an anaesthetic it would probably die. Unlike humans, dolphins don't breathe on auto pilot and need to stay conscious at all times.

A dolphin's flipper has five digits and the same structure as a human hand.

Although dolphins are a bald mammal, they are born with some hair on their snouts which falls out 2 weeks after their birth.

Scientists believe dolphins can only see in shades of grey rather than colour.

While we know dolphins are intelligent, scientists can't really be sure just how clever they really are?

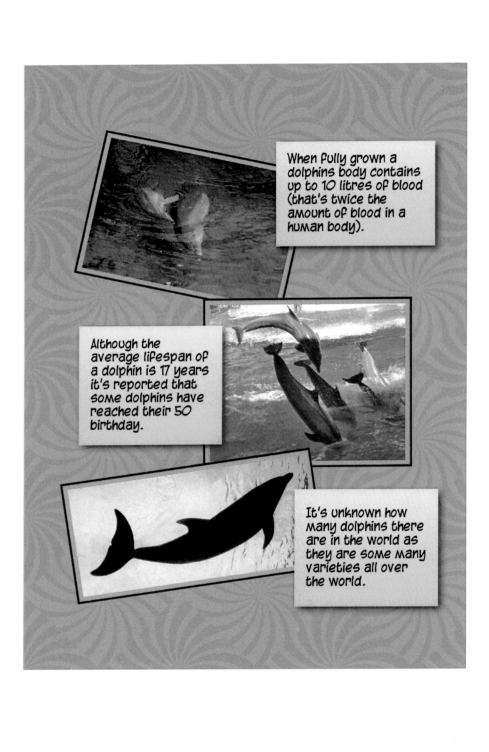

When fully grown a dolphins body contains up to 10 litres of blood (that's twice the amount of blood in a human body).

Although the average lifespan of a dolphin is 17 years it's reported that some dolphins have reached their 50 birthday.

It's unknown how many dolphins there are in the world as they are some many varieties all over the world.

While you might think that sharks are dolphin's most feared enemy, human beings are more dangerous to their lifestyle and existence.

Dolphins shed their skin constantly. This helps to reduce bacteria and other "nasty's" that stick to them.

Dolphins can call out to each individual dolphin with a unique whistle. Apart from humans it doesn't seem like any other animal that does this.

When dolphins swim in grounds the females are always at the centre of the group. The male dolphins swim at their sides to protect against shark attack and other dangers.

The deepest ever dolphin dive on record is 300M underwater by a Navy dolphin called "Tuffy".

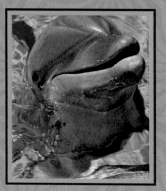

Dolphins will work with other sea creatures and even humans to get food.

Baby dolphins swim alongside their mums. By doing this they get pulled along in her current and don't need to spend much energy swimming to keep up.

Dolphins make all their sounds through their blow hole rather than with their mouth.

A "Killer Whale" isn't actually a whale but a dolphin.

Amazon River dolphins are pink in colour rather than the usual grey we're familiar with.

Pink dolphins seem to get "pinker" when they're excited or surprised.

Dolphins can hear up to 10 times better than humans.

Dolphin's breast milk contains up to 33% fat which helps the baby dolphins to put on weight very quickly.

Dolphins have two stomachs, one which they use for feeding and the other which they use for digestion.

Dolphins sleep with one eye open.

Anyone killing a dolphin in ancient Greek times was punished with death.

Rather than having one partner through their lifetime, dolphins can have many partners and mate all year round.

Dolphin's teeth look like sharp round cones.

Dolphins can only breathe through their blow hole and not through their mouths.

While its hard to believe, dolphins used to originally live on land and looked like a small wolf.

Dolphins have been trained by the navy to sniff out and detect bombs and mines under water.

A dolphin's brain can weigh up to 1800 grams (that's heavier than a human brain).

When a female dolphin is about to give birth she has a "Midwife" dolphin who helps her with the birthing process. All the other dolphins in the pod circle around for protection while the mother is giving birth.

A fully grown dolphin can eat 30 pounds of fish a day.

A dolphin can swim at speeds of up to 25 miles per hour.

A dolphin's tail is called a "Fluke".

It's unknown how many dolphins there are in the world as they are some many varieties all over the world.

In ancient Rome it was thought that dolphins carried people's souls to the "Islands of the Blest".

While dolphins have great eye sight and hearing they have a poor sense of smell.

Dolphins "sonar" is even better than that of bats or any ever made by man.

Dolphins can understand up to 60 words.

Baby dolphins are born tail first so they don't drown at birth.

Dolphins have the ability to taste sweet, sour and salty foods.

Female dolphin usually have only one baby (calf) at a time. It's very rare for a dolphin to have twins.

Some young dolphins stay with their mother until they've reached their 8 birthday.

It's believed that dolphins can use their high pitched sounds to stun fish before they catch them.

And finally, dolphins have been known to help fishermen by herding fish into their nets.

WANT TO KNOW MORE?...

Check out our great titles on Amazon.com

"Cool Facts About Cats"

"Cool Facts About Dogs"

"Cool Facts About Horses"

Made in the USA
Middletown, DE
15 December 2014